What Do ARCHAEOLOGISTS Do?

CAREERS IN SCIENCE

BENJAMIN PROUDFIT

PowerKiDS press

NEW YORK

Published in 2022 by The Rosen Publishing Group, Inc.
29 East 21st Street, New York, NY 10010

Copyright © 2022 by The Rosen Publishing Group, Inc.

All rights reserved. No part of this book may be reproduced in any form without permission in writing from the publisher, except by a reviewer.

First Edition

Portions of this work were originally authored by Mark Harasymiw and published as *Be an Archaeologist!* All new material in this edition was authored by Benjamin Proudfit.

Editor: Kristen Rajczak Nelson
Book Design: Michael Flynn

Photo Credits: Cover FCG/Shutterstock.com; (background texture) Anna Timoshenko/Shutterstock.com; p. 5 W. Scott McGill/Shutterstock.com; p. 7 AFP/Stringer/Getty Images; p. 8 Nikolay Kristakiev/Shutterstock.com; p. 9 Owen Humphreys/PA Images/Getty Images; p. 10 Ary6/E+/Getty Images; p. 11 DHuss/E+/Getty Images; p. 13 The Washington Post/Getty Images; p. 14 microgen/iStock/Getty Images; p. 15 Boston Globe/Getty Images; p. 16 claudiodivizia/iStock/Getty Images; p. 17 AFP/Stringer/Getty Images; p. 19 dndavis/iStock/Getty Images; p. 20 Hulton Archive/Getty Images; p. 21 Jeff J. Mitchell/Getty Images; p. 23 HAYKIRDI/iStock/Getty Images; p. 25 (main) Edmond Terakopian/Getty Images; p. 25 (inset) Leemage/Corbis Historical/Getty Images; p. 26 Hannes Magerstaedt/Stringer/Getty Images; p. 27 Apic/Hulton Archive/Getty Images; p. 29 Paul Biris/Moment/Getty Images.

Library of Congress Cataloging-in-Publication Data

Names: Proudfit, Benjamin, author.
Title: What do archaeologists do? / Benjamin Proudfit.
Description: New York : PowerKids Press, [2022] | Series: Careers in
  science | Includes bibliographical references and index.
Identifiers: LCCN 2020040292 | ISBN 9781725329478 (library binding) | ISBN
  9781725329454 (paperback) | ISBN 9781725329461 (6 pack)
Subjects: LCSH: Archaeologists--Juvenile literature. |
  Archaeology--Juvenile literature.
Classification: LCC CC107 .P76 2022 | DDC 930.1--dc23
LC record available at https://lccn.loc.gov/2020040292

Manufactured in the United States of America

Some of the images in this book illustrate individuals who are models. The depictions do not imply actual situations or events.

CPSIA Compliance Information: Batch #CSPK22. For further information contact Rosen Publishing, New York, New York at 1-800-237-9932.

CONTENTS

A PEEK INTO THE PAST 4
BECOMING AN ARCHAEOLOGIST 6
TIME TO DIG IN 10
LEARNING FROM FINDS .16
FAMOUS ARCHAEOLOGICAL FINDS 24
LOOK TO THE PAST, LOOK TO THE FUTURE 28
GLOSSARY 30
FOR MORE INFORMATION 31
INDEX. 32

A PEEK INTO THE PAST

Some of what's known about human history comes from written records. But, what about the ancient **civilizations** that were around before written records? Others may have records that were lost over time. Today, scientists discover their stories by studying the artifacts left behind. The study of artifacts and features left behind by people is called archaeology. The scientists who do this study are called archaeologists.

Archaeology is part of anthropology, which is the study of humans. Archaeologists work to understand how people lived in the past. They can find out what kinds of homes a civilization built and whether they had tools for hunting or farming. By looking at artifacts and features in an area, archaeologists can place more pieces in the puzzle of human history!

WHAT'S AN ARTIFACT?

An object that's small enough to be moved or carried, such as a piece of pottery, is called an artifact. An object too big to move, like a pyramid, is called a feature. Archaeologists study both of these types of man-made objects and try to figure out how, when, and why they were made and used.

Artifacts, such as these arrowheads, are objects that are made by people. They can include pottery, art, or tools. Artifacts may be found whole, or more likely, broken into pieces.

BECOMING AN ARCHAEOLOGIST

Before archaeologists can head out to find amazing artifacts, they have to learn a lot. Archaeologists commonly go to college and study anthropology. They must also study a lot of history, but all of human history is a huge subject! Those studying to be archaeologists will choose what time period in history they want to investigate and learn all they can about it.

Science classes are equally important for future archaeologists. Some colleges have an archaeology lab or a museum that offers training and work opportunities. Mastering a foreign language is also useful, as archaeologists often travel around the world!

MORE SCHOOL?

Many archaeologists continue their studies after college. They may earn a master's degree or even a doctorate, which is the highest level of degree in the United States. This takes many years. It often includes working in the field with established anthropologists and archaeologists to gain hands-on skills and knowledge.

Archaeologists often use advanced archaeology students as part of their team at a dig site, or the place where archaeologists look for artifacts.

Archaeologists not only have to choose a time period to study, but also whether they want to be one of the special kinds of archaeologists. A historical archaeologist works with both the artifacts found at a dig site and historical **documents** from a certain time or place. Geoarchaeologists connect geology, or the study of rocks, with archaeology. They study how land has changed over time and how people have been part of that.

Underwater archaeologists work in much the same way as archaeologists who work on land. They just do it underwater, studying shipwrecks, downed airplanes, and more. They find artifacts having to do with wars fought on water and learn ways that people have spent time on and in the water.

Archaeologists found an underwater settlement near northern England that could be 10,000 years old!

TIME TO DIG IN

Archaeologists are best known for one part of their job: excavation. Excavate means to dig up. But how do they know where to start? First, they decide on a question they want answered. Perhaps there's an ancient city they read about and no one knows what happened to it!

Archaeologists might match ancient maps to modern maps to find out where to start looking. They may see odd features in photographs taken from airplanes or by **satellites**. These may suggest people long ago changed the landscape.

Sometimes finding a dig site is just an accident! People digging holes for other reasons, such as farmers and construction workers, may come across buried artifacts and features.

victim of Mount Vesuvius

BURIED TREASURE!

Sand, dust, soil, and mud can build up over artifacts and features over hundreds or even thousands of years. Sometimes entire locations become hidden from view because of natural events, such as **volcanic eruptions**. People may have covered sites too! Sometimes, many different structures are built in the same place over hundreds of years. Artifacts of the earlier peoples may be found buried under or around these sites.

The ancient city of Pompeii and all the people who lived there were buried by the volcanic eruption of Mount Vesuvius in 79 CE.

11

Once a site has been chosen, archaeologists have to get permission to start digging from the government or a landowner. The next step is to make maps of the site and take many photographs before the digging starts. The excavation will change the look of the land, so it's important to record how it looked originally.

Archaeologists survey, or look over, the area. Sometimes, clues—like pieces of broken pottery—are found aboveground and show a good place to get started. Archaeologists then divide the dig site into a **grid** to help them remember where artifacts were found. Slowly and carefully, archaeologists begin to remove dirt, sand, and stone to find what's underneath.

STAYING ORGANIZED

Everything that's found in an archaeological dig is photographed in the ground before it's removed. It's put in a bag with similar things found in the same square of the grid, called a provenience. Everything is cataloged, or recorded, including what it looks like, where it was found, and what else it was found near.

Archaeological sites are often large and a dig will only excavate a small part of it.

Archaeologists use many different kinds of tools in their work. You might guess the most common archaeological tools used on a dig: shovels, brooms, and brushes. Archaeologists also use **sieves**. These tools are handy to find tiny artifacts that can be missed when digging through lots of dirt and sand. Lots of buckets to hold extra dirt are useful. Plastic sheets are brought to a dig site to protect the site if it rains.

Digs can take years, and it costs a lot to keep a dig going. Often, archaeologists leave parts of the excavation site untouched. This is also so future archaeologists who have better tools and more knowledge can search the site.

Archaeologists are thorough because they never know what information can be learned now or by future scientists. Even the soil where artifacts are found is saved to test for chemicals or other matter.

LEARNING FROM FINDS

Even though working at a dig site is exciting, it's not the biggest part of an archaeologist's job. Archaeologists spend a lot of time working in a lab, studying what they find during a dig.

Archaeologists and other scientists work to figure out the age of the artifacts they've found. Some objects are easy to date, especially if the date is found on the object itself. This is called self-dating. This sometimes occurs with items like coins. Knowing the date of an item like a coin can help date an object found right next to it on the dig. That's called relative dating.

A scientist can learn the age of bone, shell, and wood objects by measuring how much **radioactive** carbon in them has broken down. Carbon dating can identify the age of artifacts up to 50,000 years old!

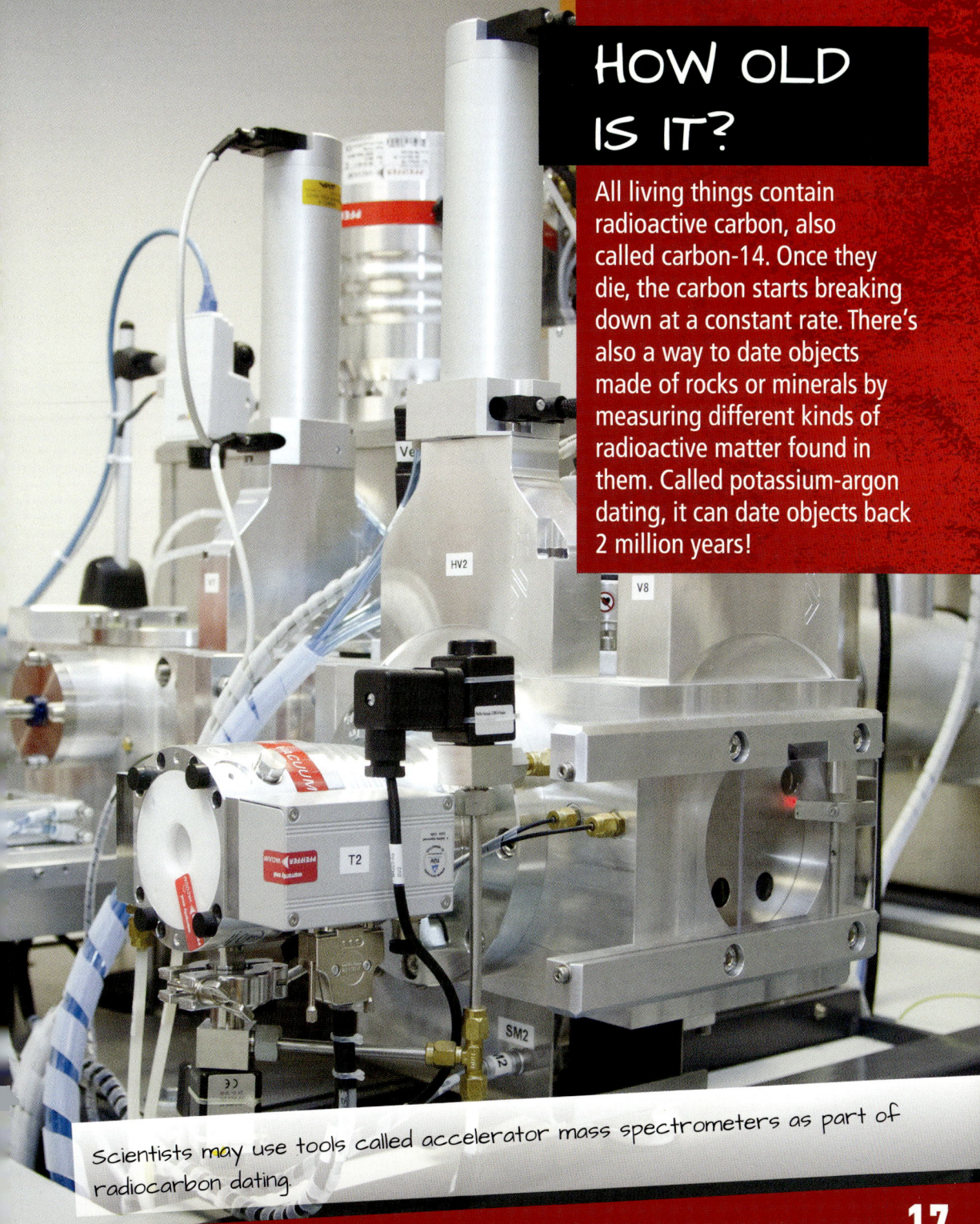

HOW OLD IS IT?

All living things contain radioactive carbon, also called carbon-14. Once they die, the carbon starts breaking down at a constant rate. There's also a way to date objects made of rocks or minerals by measuring different kinds of radioactive matter found in them. Called potassium-argon dating, it can date objects back 2 million years!

Scientists may use tools called accelerator mass spectrometers as part of radiocarbon dating.

Once an artifact has been dated and its **details** have been recorded, archaeologists try to figure out how and why it was used. They consider the ways objects found together might have something to do with one another.

This part of an archaeologist's job is called interpretation. They use the facts they've gathered and combine them with what other scientists have learned about the people and history of a place. Then, they explain what they think happened at the site and why they think the findings may be important. This interpretation is really just a good guess about what happened. It's a lot like piecing together a story without knowing all the facts. Many objects were probably destroyed before an archaeologist could study the site.

In 1974, Chinese farmers discovered the tomb of the first Chinese emperor. Inside, archaeologists found thousands of terra-cotta soldiers and horses. It gave historians new information about ancient China!

Archaeologists don't work on their interpretations alone. They work with other types of **experts** such as metallurgists and conservators. Metallurgists are scientists who study metals and can help archaeologists identify what kinds of metals are in an artifact. Conservators are specialists trained in repairing and caring for objects so they're not damaged by light or air.

Collaboration, or working together, is a big part of being a successful archaeologist. This is particularly true because archaeologists often have other responsibilities than just going on digs and looking at artifacts. They work at museums and colleges around the world. They help teach students and the public about human history.

William Wallace

ARTIFACT LIBRARY

Artifacts are often kept in museum collections with other items from an area or time period. Scientists and historians, as well as curious visitors, can get a picture of what life was like then. What's on display isn't all a museum has though. They often have thousands of other artifacts in storage!

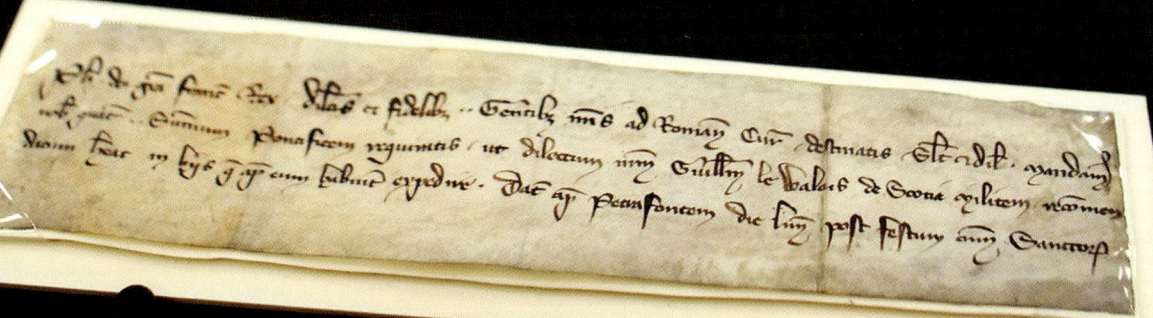

All kinds of artifacts can be found in museums. This 700-year-old letter may have been given to the Scottish hero William Wallace!

Archaeologists are scientists, but they need to be writers too. They write out their findings and interpretation and **publish** it. They want to spread the word about anything exciting they've discovered to both other scientists and the public. Other archaeologists are interested in the findings so they can use the information in their own work. These publications also allow people who aren't scientists to learn what archaeologists have found out about human history.

In addition, archaeologists have to write about what kinds of work they would like to do next. They commonly need to apply for money from a college or government program in order to set up their next dig, get new tools, or plan programs in their community about archaeology.

Archaeologists spend a long time working on pieces of writing they want to publish. They start taking notes as soon as they begin work at a dig site!

FAMOUS ARCHAEOLOGICAL FINDS

Archaeology came into the spotlight in 1799, when a wall in the Egyptian town of Rosetta was found. The stone was dated March 27 in the year 196 BCE. It featured three different kinds of writing: ancient Greek, **demotic script**, and hieroglyphics, an ancient Egyptian writing system that used symbols and pictures. Experts from different countries raced to be the first to figure out its meaning.

By 1802, the Greek and demotic sections were **translated**. No one knew what each hieroglyph meant, however. One scholar, Jean-François Champollion, was able to crack the code in 1822 by identifying certain words in the hieroglyphic section that corresponded with the same words in the Greek and demotic sections. He was soon able to translate the whole hieroglyphic section.

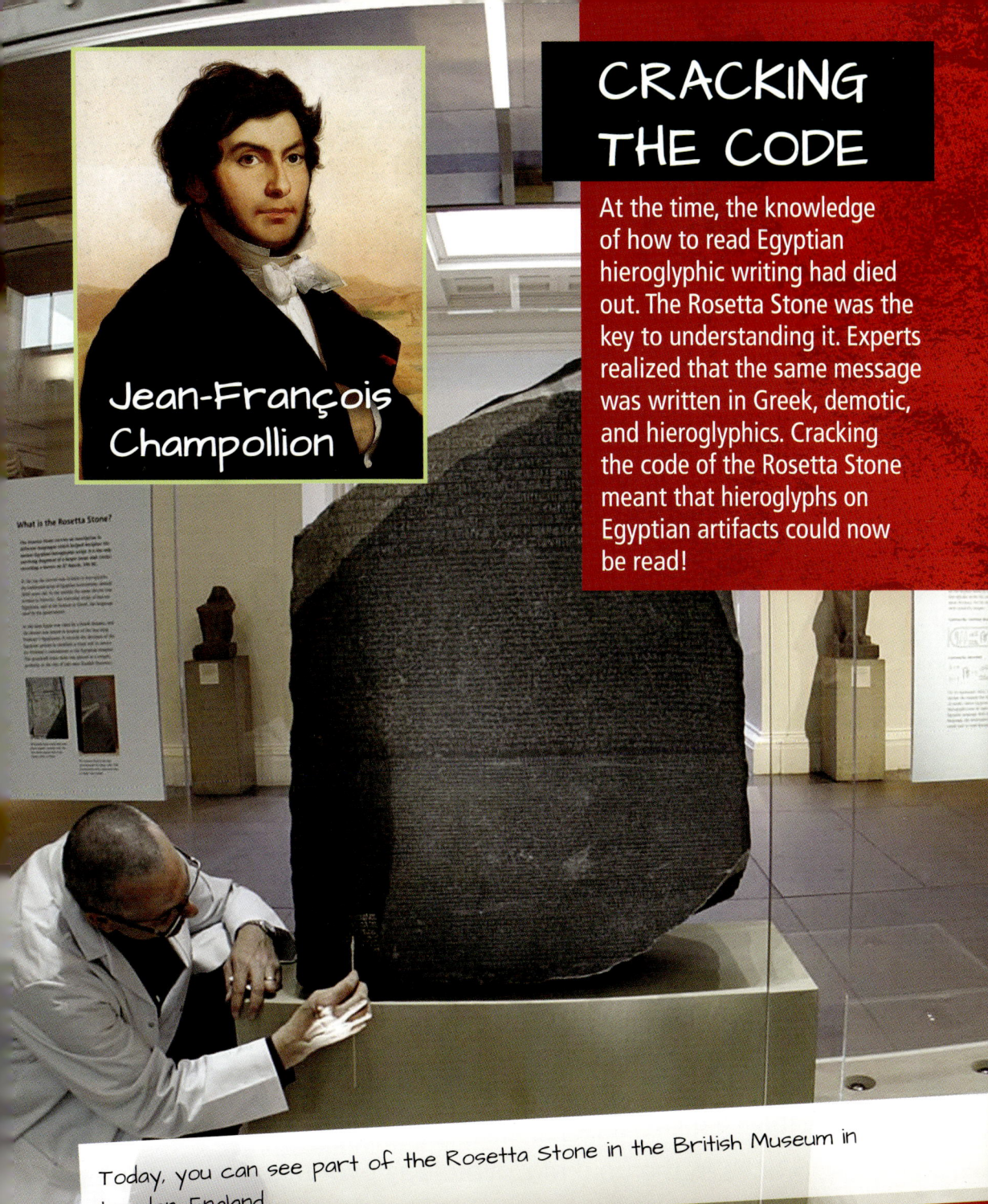

Jean-François Champollion

CRACKING THE CODE

At the time, the knowledge of how to read Egyptian hieroglyphic writing had died out. The Rosetta Stone was the key to understanding it. Experts realized that the same message was written in Greek, demotic, and hieroglyphics. Cracking the code of the Rosetta Stone meant that hieroglyphs on Egyptian artifacts could now be read!

Today, you can see part of the Rosetta Stone in the British Museum in London, England.

Howard Carter was a British archaeologist who found the tombs of many ancient Egyptian pharaohs. In 1922, Carter made his most famous discovery in Egypt's Valley of the Kings: the tomb of King Tutankhamun, often called King Tut. This was one of the most important archaeological discoveries in the field of Egyptology ever made!

Unlike other Egyptian tombs, robbers hadn't broken in and stolen the tomb's riches. Carter and his companions found King Tut's solid gold coffin and golden mask. Inside the coffin was Tut's mummy. Many other artifacts were found, including couches, thrones, vases, and chests—all partly covered in gold! It took 10 years for Carter and his team to carefully empty King Tut's tomb so it could all be studied.

Howard Carter (left), shown here with King Tut's mummy, also found the tombs of Egyptian rulers Hatshepsut and Thutmose IV.

LOOK TO THE PAST, LOOK TO THE FUTURE

Archaeologists study the past, but their work always looks to the future. They leave parts of archaeological sites untouched in order for better excavation to occur in the future. They allow their findings to be viewed by other scientists and the public in publications and museums. This invites future interpretation of their work.

Would you like to be an archaeologist? Becoming one of these curious scientists takes many years of careful study. However, having an open mind and lots of creativity are important parts of archaeology too! If you want to help put together pieces of the puzzle of human history, this field is for you!

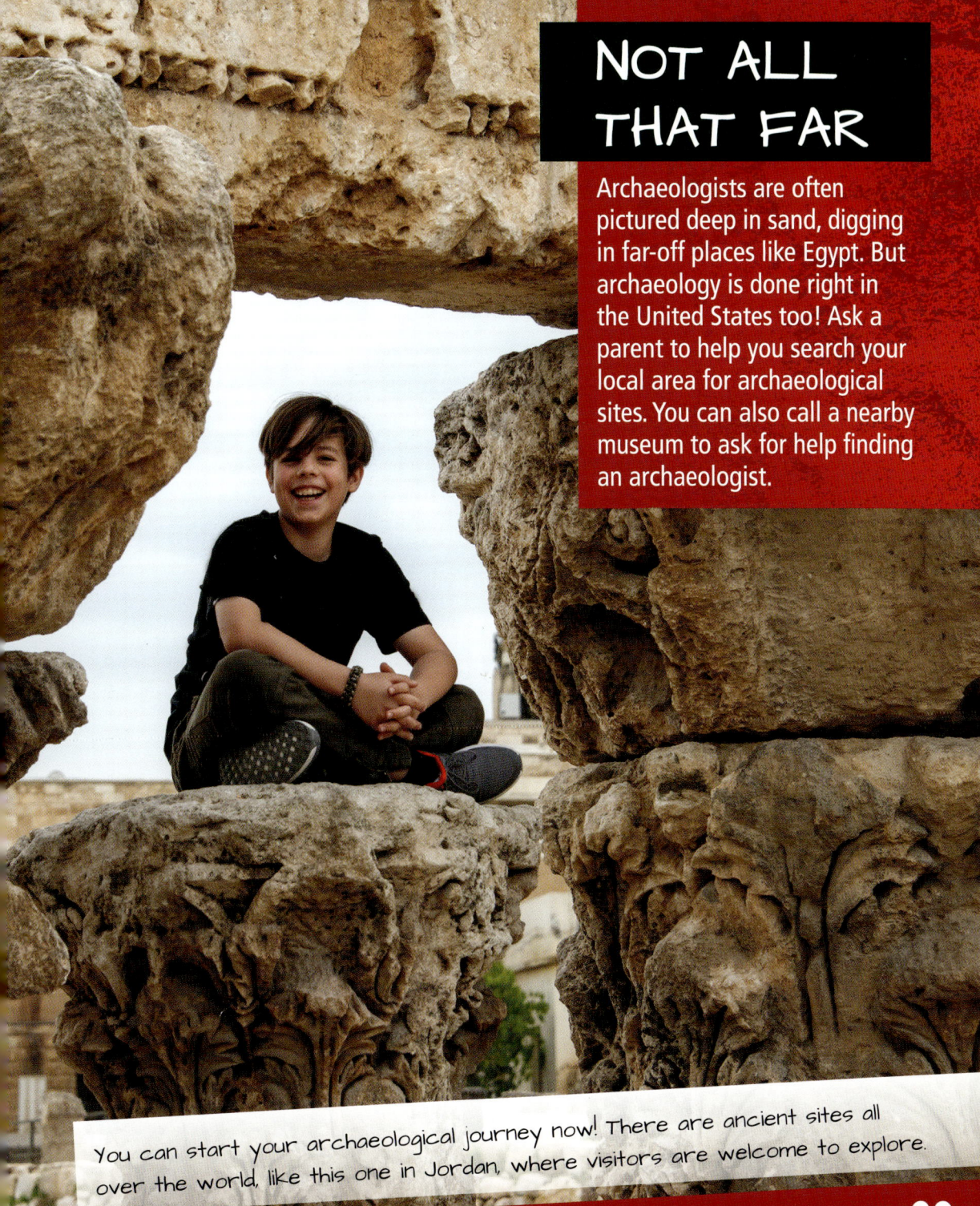

NOT ALL THAT FAR

Archaeologists are often pictured deep in sand, digging in far-off places like Egypt. But archaeology is done right in the United States too! Ask a parent to help you search your local area for archaeological sites. You can also call a nearby museum to ask for help finding an archaeologist.

You can start your archaeological journey now! There are ancient sites all over the world, like this one in Jordan, where visitors are welcome to explore.

29

GLOSSARY

civilization: An organized society with written records and laws.

demotic script: An ancient Egyptian form of writing often used when recording documents.

detail: A small part of something.

document: A formal piece of writing.

expert: Someone who knows a great deal about something.

grid: A set of squares formed by crisscrossing lines.

publish: To have something you wrote included in a book, magazine, or newspaper.

radioactive: Putting out harmful energy in the form of tiny particles.

satellite: An object that circles Earth in order to collect and send information or aid in communication.

sieve: A tool used to separate large bits of matter from smaller bits of matter or solids from liquids.

translate: To change words from one language to another.

volcanic eruption: The bursting forth of hot, liquid rock from within Earth.

For More Information

Books

Romero, Libby. *What Is an Archaeologist?* Washington, D.C.: National Geographic, 2019.

Thomas, Rachael L. *Uncovering Ancient Artifacts.* North Mankato, MN: Checkboard Library, 2019.

Websites

Archaeology for Kids
www.nps.gov/archeology/public/kids/index.htm
This website from the National Park Service will make you an archaeology expert!

What Is Archaeology?
amnh.org/explore/ology/archaeology
Learn all about archaeology and do cool archaeological activities on this site.

Publisher's note to educators and parents: Our editors have carefully reviewed these websites to ensure that they are suitable for students. Many websites change frequently, however, and we cannot guarantee that a site's future contents will continue to meet our high standards of quality and educational value. Be advised that students should be closely supervised whenever they access the Internet.

INDEX

A
anthropology, 4, 6

C
college, 6, 7, 20, 22

D
dating, 16, 17, 18

E
excavation, 10, 12, 15, 28

G
geoarchaeologists, 8
grid, 12, 13

H
historical archaeologist, 8

I
interpretation, 18, 20, 22, 28

K
King Tut, 26, 27

L
lab, 6, 16

M
museum, 6, 20, 21, 28, 29

P
Pompeii, 11
provenience, 12

R
Rosetta Stone, 24, 25

S
survey, 12

T
tools, 4, 5, 14, 15, 17, 22

U
underwater archaeologists, 9